SRA Art
Connections

# Artist Profiles

## Level 2

**SRA
McGraw-Hill**

*Columbus, Ohio*

*A Division of The McGraw·Hill Companies*

**Cover: André Derain.** (French). *The Turning Road, L'Estaque*. 1906. Oil on canvas. $51 \times 76\frac{3}{4}$ inches. Museum of Fine Arts, Houston, Texas. The John A. and Audrey Jones Beck Collection.

*SRA/McGraw-Hill*

*A Division of The **McGraw·Hill** Companies*

Send all inquiries to:
SRA/McGraw-Hill
250 Old Wilson Bridge Road
Suite 310
Worthington, OH  43085

Printed in the United States of America.

ISBN 0-02-688340-6

1 2 3 4 5 6 7 8 9 POH 01 00 99 98 97

# Table of Contents

# Thomas Affleck (tom´ əs af´ lek)
*(1740–1795)*

## About the Artist

Thomas Affleck was born in Scotland, learned to make cabinets in London, and migrated to America. In 1763, Governor Penn asked Affleck to leave London and make cabinets for him and other families in Philadelphia. The Revolution began soon afterward. When he returned, he became the wealthiest cabinetmaker in Philadelphia. He built furniture for many government offices. After Affleck's death, his son continued to build furniture for a while, but the business ended in bankruptcy.

## ABOUT ART HISTORY

Affleck was known as the maker of Philadelphia Chippendale-style furniture. He had a copy of *The Gentleman and Cabinet-Maker's Director* by Thomas Chippendale, and he used Chippendale's elaborate designs. Those designs include legs with claw-and-ball feet and a lot of detailed carving. In time, Affleck simplified the English designs so they became uniquely American. Some of his later pieces show his interpretation of the sturdy Neo-classical style of furniture.

## ABOUT THE ARTIST'S WORK

Some of Affleck's furniture has been lost or destroyed, but the pieces that remain

*Thomas Affleck. (American).* Sidechair. *1770. Mahogany, white cedar, 20th century silk damask upholstery. $36\frac{7}{8} \times 21\frac{7}{8} \times 18\frac{3}{8}$ inches. Philadelphia Museum of Art, Philadelphia, Pennsylvania. Gift of Robert L. McNeil, Jr.*

include chairs, desks, bookcases, and several kinds of chests.

## ABOUT THE MEDIA

Affleck worked mainly in mahogany, the wood preferred for Chippendale furniture, but he also used oak, cedar, and other types of wood.

## ABOUT THE TECHNIQUE

Affleck could make a heavy piece of furniture seem so light that it seemed like it was "dancing to eighteenth-century music." By choosing certain grains of wood and by using carvings that attracted viewers' attention, he could make a large cabinet seem delicate. Affleck also carefully planned the proportions of each piece so that everything was harmonious.

## About the Artist

Suad al-Attar was born in Baghdad, Iraq, in 1942. She studied art, with a concentration in printmaking, in the United States, London, and Iraq. In 1964, she became the first Iraqi woman ever to have a solo exhibition of her artwork. Since then, she has had many one-woman shows in the Middle East; London; Los Angeles; and Washington, DC. She has also won many awards and prizes for her artwork. Her art is in museum collections worldwide. She lives and works in London, England.

### ABOUT ART HISTORY

In honor of their ancestry, some Arabic artists use ancient, traditional elements in their works. Examples of these elements include calligraphy and traditional geometric designs.

### ABOUT THE ARTWORK

al-Attar's artwork is filled with symbolism and patterns. She usually shows one or two stylized figures standing or lying on the ground. The sky is dark and sometimes shows a moon or stars. The ground is often covered with vines, flowers, or leaves. Sometimes al-Attar uses rows of Islamic calligraphy to cover the earth. The figures seem to be examining the world around them as they look up at the sky or into the distance.

*Courtesy Suad al-Attar*

### ABOUT THE MEDIA

al-Attar creates her prints with ink on paper. Her drawings are made with pen on paper. She also paints with oil paints on canvas.

### ABOUT THE TECHNIQUE

al-Attar creates mood in her fantasy images by mixing many patterns together. The figures she shows have organic, flowing forms. These forms are then filled with geometric patterns. Sometimes more than one pattern or texture will fill a form. She prefers to use dark backgrounds. al-Attar accentuates her oil paintings with splashes of rich, bright colors such as gold and green.

# Romare Bearden (rōmär´ bēr´ dən)
## *(1914–1988)*

## About the Artist

Bearden was born in North Carolina. His family moved to Harlem in New York City when he was three years old. His family's home became a meeting place for artists, writers, and musicians during the Harlem Renaissance. Still, Bearden studied math, not the arts, in college. But he worked as a cartoonist and illustrator to pay for it. When he was 21, he decided to become an artist. Over the years, Bearden studied art in New York City and in Paris. He also worked as a social worker, served in the army, and wrote several songs and books. Bearden was known as a warm-hearted and friendly man. His wife was also an artist as well as a dancer.

### ABOUT ART HISTORY

Bearden experimented with abstract expressionism. He later developed his own style and created collages combining painting and photographs. He often showed his subjects at odd angles, in a style similar to Cubism.

### ABOUT THE ARTWORK

Bearden focused much of his work on African American life. His choice of subjects also was inspired by the legends of Homer, jazz and other music, and religion. Bearden's later paintings show scenes and colors from the West Indies. His wife's family lived there, and the Beardens often visited.

*Courtesy of the Romare Bearden Foundation and VAGA, New York, NY*

### ABOUT THE MEDIA

Bearden was a painter and a printmaker. Bearden began by painting with tempera on brown paper, the kind used for grocery bags. Later, he also used watercolors, oils, and acrylics. He incorporated photographic images in his paintings.

### ABOUT THE TECHNIQUE

Bearden was a painter and printmaker. Some of Bearden's paintings included magazine photographs pieced together like a quilt. Other times, he painted on several layers of rice paper. Then, he tore away some sections and added others. He continued to tear and paint until he had created the picture he wanted.

## About the Artist

This native of Columbus, Ohio, showed an early talent for both drawing and athletics. After several years at The Ohio State University, where he made sketches for the yearbook and the student newspaper, Bellows left college to play semiprofessional baseball. His baseball earnings, plus the sale of several drawings, enabled him to go to New York and study art. He lived in an apartment across the street from Sharkey's, a prize-fighting club that became the setting of his famous painting *Stag at Sharkey's.* Restless and ambitious, he was always ready to try new projects and techniques. By the time he was 28, top collectors were buying his paintings and, later, his lithographs. Bellows married his college sweetheart and had two daughters. He died suddenly at age 42 of a ruptured appendix.

### ABOUT ART HISTORY

Bellows is part of the "Ashcan School" of painting. At the New York School of Art, he studied under Robert Henri, who sent his students into the street to observe reality and beauty in the urban scene. Not interested in studying art in France or Italy, Bellows was an American Realist.

### ABOUT THE ARTWORK

In his short life, Bellows managed to finish more than 600 oil paintings and thousands of drawings and lithographs. Some of his art focused on the violence in boxing. *Both Members of the Club* shows two fierce,

*Corbis*

sweaty, bloody boxers. He also painted sensitive portraits and seascapes and cityscapes full of movement and energy.

### ABOUT THE MEDIA

This artist worked in oils and lithographs.

### ABOUT THE TECHNIQUE

Bellows' early paintings were marked by slashing brush strokes and had a dark, smokey look that captured the mood of illegal prize-fighting clubs. Later in his career, Bellows began to use a geometrical formula to compose his human figures. Some thought this approach took the life out of his paintings.

# Thomas Hart Benton (tom´ əs härt bent´ən)
## (1889 – 1975)

## About the Artist

Thomas Hart Benton was a regionalist American painter known for his energetic, colorful murals. He was the son of a United States congressman and named after his great uncle, the famous pre-American Civil War Senator. From his family, Benton developed a strong identity as an American. Benton studied art at the Art Institute of Chicago and in Paris. He believed that American artists should develop their own styles and not just copy French painting styles. Although Benton began his art career as a cartoonist, he was well-known for his murals depicting scenes from the rural past of the American South and Southwest.

*Corbis-Bettmann*

## ABOUT ART HISTORY

Benton painted subjects from mostly one region—the American Midwest. He helped develop and promote the American art style known as regionalism. He urged American artists to paint scenes from the lives of ordinary Americans. He also encouraged his students to try new ideas in their artwork. One of his students was the well-known painter Jackson Pollock.

## ABOUT THE ARTWORK

Benton enjoyed painting Midwestern farm scenes. Many of his paintings show sunburned farmers and huge work horses. In *Cradling Wheat,* several farmers and one of their sons are shown harvesting wheat by hand. Benton's paintings remind viewers of days gone by in rural America.

## ABOUT THE MEDIA

Along with other media, Benton used oil and egg tempera.

## ABOUT THE TECHNIQUE

Benton used his experience as a cartoonist in his later paintings. In some, he divided scenes with borders, like a comic strip.

# Paul Cézanne (paul sā zän´)
## (1839–1906)

## About the Artist

Cézanne was born in Aix-en-Provence, in the south of France. He is often called the father of modern art. He loved to paint, but people did not like his work very much. He had to beg gallery owners to show his work, and therefore he did not sell very many paintings. He inherited money from his parents to pay his bills and buy his paints. He kept painting until a week before he died.

## ABOUT ART HISTORY

Cézanne is called a Post-Impressionist. He was greatly influenced by the painter Camille Pissarro. Pissaro introduced Cézanne to the new Impressionist technique for capturing outdoor light. People did not think much of Cézanne's work while he was alive. Cézanne combined Impressionism with a formal instruction the Impressionists had abandoned. He looked very closely at things to find their basic forms and shapes. He painted cylinders, spheres, and cones to show these forms. Sometimes he changed the shapes he saw in nature to make his paintings more interesting. Picasso, Matisse, and other artists studied Cézanne's ideas.

## ABOUT THE ARTWORK

Cézanne painted landscapes, still lifes, and portraits. Many of his landscapes were of the countryside and mountains near his home.

*Scala/Art Resource, NY*

He developed a unique way of representing nature and objects in a highly creative and abstract fashion. Cézanne painted slowly, often taking several days to create a still life. One friend posed 115 times so Cézanne could finish his portrait.

## ABOUT THE MEDIA

Cézanne worked in both oils and watercolor.

## ABOUT THE TECHNIQUE

Cézanne used bright colors and bold brush strokes, especially in the skies of his landscapes. He applied the paint in vertical and horizontal lines. He knew that cool colors seem to pull back and warm colors seem to go forward. He used this knowledge to make his paintings seem three-dimensional. Cézanne also used different shades of the same color to add shape to his subjects; for example, to make an apple look round and not flat.

# Patrick Des Jarlait (pat´ rik dā zhär lā)
## (1912–1972)

## About the Artist

Des Jarlait was born at Red Lake Indian Reservation in Minnesota. Growing up, he learned the traditions of the Chippewa, also called the Anishinabe and the Ojibwe. From the age of five, Des Jarlait loved to paint, sketch, and draw. He studied art in high school and at Arizona State College. He served in the navy during World War II. When he returned home, he continued to paint. He also gave talks to students about his Native American heritage.

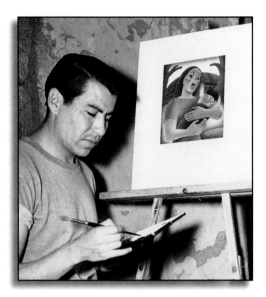

*San Diego Historical Society,
Union Tribune Collection*

### ABOUT ART HISTORY
Des Jarlait belonged to the Red Lake Chippewa. He painted their traditions and customs to help preserve their way of life. Des Jarlait did not become famous while he was alive. But today many people consider his paintings important to the development of Midwestern Native American art.

### ABOUT THE ARTWORK
Des Jarlait's paintings are stunning with their bold shapes and bright colors. The faces of people in his paintings are usually very angular. He often painted Native Americans dancing, preparing food, or caring for children. Many of his paintings tell detailed stories about the Chippewa way of life and reflect their respect for the land.

### ABOUT THE MEDIA
This artist usually painted with watercolors.

### ABOUT THE TECHNIQUE
Des Jarlait had a very personal style. He made his people look crisp by using sharp lines for their noses, cheekbones, and jaws. He used mostly black and white to color heir eyes, which created strong contrast. He painted their clothes with bright colors, such as pink, yellow, and orange.

# Jean Dubuffet (zhän dū´ bū fā)
## (1901–1985)

## About the Artist

Dubuffet was born in France. He spent his life rebelling. As a young man, he studied art. He withdrew from the art world to take over his family business. At the age of 41, Dubuffet went back to painting and found almost immediate acceptance and success.

### ABOUT ART HISTORY

Critics described Dubuffet's style "raw art" because of its sometimes crude and violent quality. He rebelled against "good taste," which he felt reflected the standards of snobs. His goal was to create art for the common people and art that came from daily life. In rebelling against accepted standards, Dubuffet encouraged other artists to experiment with new forms and techniques.

*John Launois/Black Star*

he called "Hourloupe." It combined painting and sculpture. It consisted of shapes covered with script or doodles. Through Hourloupe, Dubuffet tried to give a three-dimensional form to his mental images.

### ABOUT THE MEDIA

Many of his artworks are assemblages (a combination of found objects that are created into a three-dimensional composition).

### ABOUT THE ARTWORK

Dubuffet's early paintings included fairly realistic landscapes and portraits, but his style became more abstract over time. By the end of the 1950s, his paintings focused mostly on textures. In the 1960s, his work became more realistic again and included Paris street scenes. Then he invented a new art form

### ABOUT THE TECHNIQUE

Dubuffet worked in a very organized way. He often painted a series of pictures that focused on one theme, and he carefully dated and numbered them. For one series of paintings, Dubuffet covered a canvas with a thick paste. Then he scratched three-dimensional images into the paste. One painting in this series was titled *Landscapes of the Mind.*

# Ivan Eyre (ī´ vən ēr)
## (1935-    )

## About the Artist

Ivan Eyre was born in rural Saskatchewan, Canada. His family was extremely poor. They moved from place to place throughout Canada as his father looked for work. When Eyre was in fifth grade, he won a prize for painting. His teachers encouraged him to continue making art. He went to after-school art classes while he was in high school. After he graduated, he went to art school in Winnipeg. In 1967, the Canada Council paid for him to travel around Europe. He returned from his travels to teach in Winnipeg. He has also taught art at the University of North Dakota and the University of Manitoba.

### ABOUT ART HISTORY

Ivan Eyre is an individualist in the art world. He does not belong to or work with any groups of artists. Eyre's work is difficult to categorize, since he often crosses boundaries of style, themes, and medium.

### ABOUT THE ARTWORK

In his artwork, Eyre tries to show how poverty and misery can be overcome with happy situations. Although Eyre lived through wars, car accidents, and natural disasters, his life was more than pain, anxiety, and terror. Most of his paintings combine elements of nature with those of civilization. Distorted figures that are long, angular, and unrealistically flat appear in many of his paintings. He paints many landscapes of wooded forests. Some of these

*Photo by Phil Hossack*

appear to be seen through frames as if the viewer is looking out the window. Sharp protrusions poke out of the windowsills toward the viewer.

### ABOUT THE MEDIA

Eyre paints with acrylic and oil paints on canvases.

### ABOUT THE TECHNIQUE

Eyre paints strong, heavy lines around his figures, which seem to float on his canvases. He uses analogous colors, usually all from one color family. The landscapes he paints show wide angles, often from a bird's-eye view. His still lifes are set at unusual angles. They are often framed by either a windowsill or an imaginary, unusually shaped frame. Sometimes Eyre applies shiny glazes over parts of his acrylic paintings to accent those areas.

# Adolph Gottlieb (āˊ dolf gätˊ lēb)
## (1903–1974)

## About the Artist

The painter Adolph Gottlieb is perhaps best known as an early and outstanding member of the New York school of Abstract Expressionists. Gottlieb, a self-assured native New Yorker, studied at the Art Students League of New York before he ventured to France to study art at the age of eighteen. He traveled through France, Austria, and Germany before he returned to New York to attend Parsons School of Design, Cooper Union, and the Educational Alliance Art School. Due to health concerns, Gottlieb and his wife lived in Arizona from 1937–1938. When returning to New York, he taught at the Pratt Institute in Brooklyn, New York.

### ABOUT ART HISTORY

As an Abstract Expressionist, Gottlieb tried to show emotions in art through nontraditional means. He was influenced by contemporary psychologists Freud and Jung and by the works of primitive, cubists and surrealists artists. Gottlieb painted in two distinct styles, "pictographs" and "bursts." During his travels in France and Europe, he developed an appreciation of thirteenth- and fourteenth-century polyptychs, which influenced his pictograph style. The Burst approach was developed after Gottlieb spent time in Arizona, where the unique character of the desert inspired him to paint landscapes with radically flattened spaces.

### ABOUT THE ARTWORK

Gottlieb's series of pictographs contain grid form compartments filled with symbols

*Yousuf Karsh/Woodfin Camp & Associates*

based on fantasy and the unconscious. Included in his pictograph paintings are images of body parts, such as eyes, hands, and heads, as well as snakes, birds, fish, dots, and arrows. Gottlieb's Burst series are partial abstractions of landscapes that contain large, exploding orbs of color reminiscent of solar bodies.

### ABOUT THE MEDIA

Gottlieb painted in oil and tempera paints.

### ABOUT THE TECHNIQUE

Gottlieb used layers of paint, both oil and tempera, to create contrasting surfaces. He painted most frequently on canvas, but occasionally on burlap. For his Bursts paintings he used larger canvases and usually painted in a three-hue palette (red and black against white).

# Francisco Goya (frän sēs´ kō gō´ yä)
## (1746–1828)

## About the Artist

Goya was an innovative Spanish painter and etcher. His father was a painter and a gilder of altarpieces. His formal education began as an artist apprentice at age 14. In time, Goya became a portrait painter for the Spanish royalty. After France invaded and took over Spain, Goya kept his position as a royal portrait painter. But he was angry about Spain's loss of freedom. He expressed these feelings in such paintings as *The Third of May, 1808.* This painting shows the execution of Spanish rebels. Goya painted other scenes of the revolution, in which Spanish rebels fought against French control. In the margins of his drawings of the violence, he sometimes noted, "I saw this." Goya's personal life also contained much sadness. Only one of his many children survived childhood. Then, at age 46, the artist lost his hearing and felt isolated from others. He spent his last years in exile in France.

### ABOUT ART HISTORY
Goya said he had three teachers: Rembrandt, Velázquez, and nature. Goya took on an artistic freedom that was new for his times. He changed the style of portrait painting. He moved away from the stiff portraits that had been fashionable. Instead, he tried to show the true personalities of his subjects, including their faults. He was a forerunner of the realism movement. As a court painter, he was highly praised for his candid views of everyday Spanish life seen in his tapestry cartoons. This work revolutionized the tapestry industry. His influence was strongly felt in nineteenth- and early twentieth-century painting and printmaking.

*Erich Lessing/Art Resource, NY*

### ABOUT THE ARTWORK
Goya's first paintings, such as *The Flower Seller,* were light-hearted, graceful pictures of everyday life. Later, he painted the horrors of war. For example, *The Disasters of the War* records Napoleon's invasion of Spain in gruesome detail. Goya also painted many religious scenes.

### ABOUT THE MEDIA
This artist expressed his ideas in paintings, engravings, etchings, lithographs, frescoes, and drawings.

### ABOUT THE TECHNIQUE
His famous paintings like *Second of May* and *Third of May* are painted in thick, bold strokes of color with highlights of brilliant yellow and red.

## About the Artist

Gwathmey, Siegel and Associates, an architectural firm formed in 1968, designed and carried out the restoration and expansion of the Guggenheim Museum. This firm has received many awards and honors for the Guggenheim and for its other design and construction projects. These projects range from Harvard University's Fogg Art Museum to the Contemporary Convention Center at Disney World in Florida. Charles Gwathmey earned a master's degree in architecture at Yale and has taught at many prestigious universities. Robert Siegel received a master's degree in architecture from Harvard. Both men have won considerable recognition for their work.

## ABOUT THE ARTWORK

Gwathmey Siegel's relationship with the Guggenheim Museum began in 1982, with a study to identify possibilities for expansion and renovation. The firm suggested an addition in 1985 but did not receive approval until 1988. It faced some of the same problems and objections as Frank Lloyd Wright did in his original design. After the design was approved, the firm spent two years replacing a four-story tower with a ten-story building, creating underground space for offices, opening more of the museum to the public, and generally restoring and modernizing the facilities.

*Frank Lloyd Wright/Gwathmey, Siegel, and Associates. (American).* The Solomon R. Guggenheim Museum. *Photograph by David Heald © The Solomon R. Guggenheim Foundation, New York, New York.*

## ABOUT THE TECHNIQUE

Gwathmey Siegel aimed to preserve and expose Frank Lloyd Wright's design rather than replace it. By taking partitions and screens out of the small rotunda, for example, the architects uncovered Wright's subtle and complex design so visitors could better appreciate it. Tower galleries and terraces were situated so visitors could see Wright's original, dramatic designs, along with impressive views of Central Park and New York City.

# Dame Barbara Hepworth
(bärb´ ə rə hep´ wûrth) *(1903–1975)*

## About the Artist

This English sculptor is known for her abstract works in wood, stone, and metal. As a Yorkshire child, she took car trips through the countryside with her father. She was impressed by the contrast between the beauty of the rural areas and the grime of the industrial towns. The land became a theme that she returned to again and again in her art. After studying art and sculpture in England, Hepworth moved to Rome and then returned to England. She married twice, once to a sculptor and once to a painter. She had a son and a set of triplets. Her relationship with her children also became an important theme of her work. In 1965, she was honored by being named a Dame of the British Empire.

### ABOUT ART HISTORY
Hepworth's work was influenced early on by the sculpture of Jean Arpand Constantin Brancusi, as well as the artwork of her friend, Henry Moore. Hepworth and Moore were the most important English sculptors of their age.

### ABOUT THE ARTWORK
This artist was fascinated by relationships. In her sculpture *Mother and Child,* for example, the two figures form a single curved shape, indicating their close relationship. She expressed her love of nature in such abstract sculptures as *Wave* and *Tides II.* Hepworth's rounded forms seem to have been shaped by nature instead of a chisel. These sculptures also show her interest in the relationship between the subject and space. She hollowed out forms or pierced them with holes, so the

*Brian Seed/Black Star*

space within the sculpture is as important as the sculpture itself. Hepworth often painted the inside surfaces of her sculptures to emphasize the open spaces. She also defined the openings by stretching strings across them. Some of her sculptures are small enough to hold in a hand. Others tower twenty feet above viewers.

### ABOUT THE MEDIA
Hepworth sculpted in wood, stone, marble, alabaster, slate, copper, and bronze.

### ABOUT THE TECHNIQUE
Hepworth sketched her sculptures before carving them. For her bronze sculptures, she first made plaster models. Her works are notable for their superb finishes.

# Auguste Herbin (ō gūst´ âr´ ban)
## (1882–1960)

## About the Artist

Herbin was born in France and studied at the Ecole des Beaux Arts. Later he went to other countries to paint. In Italy, he noticed how different kinds of light made things look different. From then on, he tried to ignore little details and paint just the main part of his subject. Herbin was enthusiastic and curious. He loved his work.

*Archive Photos*

## ABOUT ART HISTORY

Herbin explored the geometric, cubist style of painting. He made the subjects in his paintings more and more simple until they were only outlines or symbols. He was very interested in shapes and colors. He studied how different colors make people feel. He also read about optical illusions and used them in some of his paintings. Herbin was an Abstract painter.

## ABOUT THE ARTWORK

Early in his career, Herbin painted large still lifes and landscapes. In time, his paintings became so symbolic that it was hard to tell what he had painted. His later pictures were brightly colored geometric shapes.

## ABOUT THE MEDIA

Herbin painted with oils.

## ABOUT THE TECHNIQUE

Herbin used flat, intense colors and bold shapes. When you look at Herbin's paintings, you cannot see the brush strokes.

## About the Artist

Wassily Kandinsky first tried painting as a teenager in his native Russia. Even then, he felt that each color had a mysterious life of its own. He was still drawn to colors and painting while he studied law and economics in college. However, at that point he believed that art was "a luxury forbidden to a Russian." In time, though, he moved to Germany, studied art, and began his career. During his life, Kandinsky moved back and forth between Russia and Germany several times. In 1933, he settled in France after Nazi storm troopers labeled his painting style "degenerate."

*Archiv/Interfoto*

## ABOUT ART HISTORY

Kandinsky was a pioneer in the pure abstract painting style: a combination of color and form with no subject matter. He did not give a title to a painting he did in 1910, but others called it the First Abstract Watercolour. Kandinsky felt that trying to paint recognizable objects distracted artists from their real jobs: expressing ideas and emotions. He believed that communicating through painting was similar to communicating with music. He often gave his paintings titles that were both musical and abstract, such as *Improvisation 30*.

## ABOUT THE ARTWORK

It's possible to identify landscapes and objects in some of Kandinsky's early paintings, but his later work was entirely abstract. Only occasionally during World War I did Kandinsky include cannons and other recognizable objects in his work.

## ABOUT THE MEDIA

Kandinsky worked in oils, watercolors, and India ink.

## ABOUT THE TECHNIQUE

Kandinsky did not try to show the "essence" of his subjects, since he had no subjects. Instead, he attempted to make forms and colors take on a meaning that was separate from the physical world. His work often impresses even viewers who are not certain what the paintings are supposed to mean.

**15**

# Suzuki Kiitsu (sū zū kē   kē ēt sū)
## (1796–1858)

## About the Artist

Suzuki Kiitsu was one of the most important masters of the Rimpa school of Japanese art. Kiitsu's father was a professional textile dyer who was well known for inventing a method of dying cloth purple. Kiitsu became interested in art because of his father. His success as an artist came partly from his relationship with the Sakai family. When he turned 18, he was accepted by Hoitsu, a famous artist and member of the Sakai family, as a pupil. Hoitsu trained Kiitsu, arranged his marriage, and saw that he was adopted into the Sakai family. Kiitsu became a samurai in the Sakai household and was appointed the role of chamberlain. These roles gave Kiitsu status. With this status, he was allowed to continue studying art. When he grew older, he trained other artists in the Rimpa tradition.

## ABOUT ART HISTORY

Tawaraya Sotatsu was the first great painter of the Rimpa school. The Rimpa masters excelled in decorative designs of strong, expressive force. Both Sotatsu and Kiitsu were famous for the beautifully decorated screens they created.

## ABOUT THE ARTWORK

Kiitsu's subject matter varied widely. He often used birds and flowers in his artwork. His works are bold in design and not as busy as the work of his Rimpa predecessors. Kiitsu refused to copy nature exactly. He arranged elements of his artworks to form delicate patterns and designs. He was skilled

*Suzuki Kiitsu. (Japanese). Sea Shells and Plums. Edo Period, nineteenth century. Hanging scroll. Color on silk. 13⅝ × 11 inches. From the Shin'enkan Collection, Los Angeles County Museum of Art, Los Angeles, California.*

at showing atmospheric effects, such as rainfall, in his art.

## ABOUT THE MEDIA

Kiitsu painted on wood-framed screens, silk, and paper using ink and gold leaf.

## ABOUT THE TECHNIQUE

By not following the Rimpa school of art at all times, Kiitsu found that he could use a more flexible style in his artworks. His emphasis on design led him to create elements that were stiff and awkward in order to accentuate the decorative impact of design in his works. He used rich colors to heighten the patterns he created.

# Paul Klee (paul klā)
## (1879–1940)

## About the Artist

Klee was born into a musical Swiss family. His family hoped he also would become a musician. At age five, his grandmother gave him his first box of pencils. He thought of himself as an artist from then on. But he kept an interest in music. Klee played his violin for an hour nearly every morning of his life. He married a pianist.

As an adult, Klee still drew simply, like a child. Klee believed that childlike drawings were the most creative and original. He was not trying to share his ideas through his work. He just wanted to explore his imagination. Klee taught himself to paint with both hands.

### ABOUT ART HISTORY
At first, art critics ignored Klee's work. Then they realized that Klee's small, charming, playful pictures were filled with ideas and meaning. Different people see different meanings in Klee's pictures. For many people, this fact adds to the value of his pictures.

### ABOUT THE ARTWORK
Klee studied nature and often began his pictures with an image from nature. Then he would let his imagination go.

### ABOUT THE MEDIA
Klee painted with watercolors and other materials on paper, canvas, silk, linen, and

*Culver Pictures*

burlap. He liked to experiment. For example, he did one picture with black paste on burlap.

### ABOUT THE TECHNIQUE
Color was very important to Klee. He once said, "Color and I are one; I am a painter." In his watercolors, Klee used thin layers of pale color. This technique made his pictures gently shimmer, like pavement under a hot sun. Klee used color like a musician uses sound.

He tried to touch viewers' feelings. Klee said that he learned more about painting from the musicians Bach and Mozart than he did from visual artists.

# Robert Lostutter (rob´ ərt lō´ stut ər)
## (1939-    )

## About the Artist

Lostutter was born in Kansas. He attended the Art Institute of Chicago. As a young artist, he learned about drawing, painting, and glazing from other artists who were interested in technique. He learned about the ways that artists work. Lostutter thinks of painting as an art that takes a lot of work and practice.

## ABOUT ART HISTORY

Regional art is based on a certain area of the nation. It's usually created by artists who were born in that area or who are very interested in it. Regional art was once only realistic, not abstract. Artists in Chicago and Houston have helped to make "imagist" art popular. Imagist art is both regional and abstract. Lostutter is known as a Chicago Imagist. The work of the Chicago Imagists is a combination of abstract images and realism.

*Jonas Dovydenas*

masks. Others have flowers on their chests or heads. The activity in these paintings is unclear, partly because Lostutter shows only part of the figures. For example, a figure's head might be outside the painting borders. The meaning of the painting is up to the viewer to decide. Lostutter also paints prehistoric leaves and fish.

## ABOUT THE MEDIA

Lostutter paints in watercolors and oils on canvas.

## ABOUT THE ARTWORK

Most of Lostutter's work shows figures that might be acrobats. They are usually being held by hands or ropes. Both their skin and costumes seem tight, as if they were sewn on. The figures seem to hold each other back and support each other, all at the same time. Some of Lostutter's figures have birdlike heads or

## ABOUT THE TECHNIQUE

Lostutter spends a great deal of time preparing sketches and watercolors before he begins to paint. He often adds glazes or enamels to his work and then repaints. This is to get the surface texture he wants. Light plays an important part in Lostutter's paintings. It gives his figures a strange beauty.

# Herón Martínez
(ār´ ōn  mär tē´ nes) *(1918–      )*

## About the Artist

Martínez was born in Mexico and began his career by creating cooking pots, like his parents, grandparents, and great-grandparents. He played with clay since childhood, but he did not want to become a potter. To support himself and his wife, he began making clay barrels, which sold well. Growing up, Martínez listened to many myths and legends. These stories and his own creativity inspired him to create unique and beautiful pottery reflecting the myths and legends of his childhood. These days, he stays busy filling orders for sculptures requested by individuals and museums. Martínez and his wife have six children.

### ABOUT ART HISTORY
Martínez, a self-taught artist, has become one of Mexico's most extraordinary folk potters. He bases some of his designs on bits of ancient pots found near his village and others on his imagination.

### ABOUT THE ARTWORK
Perhaps Martínez's best known pieces are his clay candelabras. They begin with a central figure that supports the rest of the structure. The candle holders grow upward and

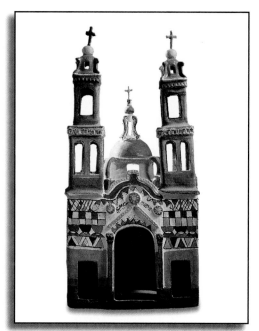

*Herón Martínez. (Mexican).* Church. *c. 1960. Painted earthenware. 24 inches high. From the Girard Foundation Collection, in the Museum of International Folk Art, a unit of the Museum of New Mexico, Santa Fe, New Mexico. Photographer: Michel Monteaux.*

outward on graceful wings. He often creates pieces in animal forms that represent the fantasies and legends of his childhood.

### ABOUT THE MEDIA
Martínez works in clay, which he sometimes finishes with polishes of different colors.

### ABOUT THE TECHNIQUE
This artist depends on his imagination for most of his designs, and also gains inspiration from religious or spiritual sources in his life.

# Claude Monet (klōd mō nāʹ)
## (1840–1926)

## About the Artist

As a young man in France, Claude Monet did not want to be a painter. He already was well paid for drawing caricatures of tourists. However, painter Eugene Boudin saw talent in Monet's exaggerated drawings and encouraged him to paint. Although artists were "supposed" to paint in studios, Boudin urged Monet to paint outside in the open air. There, Monet learned to capture his first impressions on canvas. He recorded these impressions during a long and productive life, outliving two wives. His greatest wish was to "mingle more closely with nature." By his death at 86, Monet was blinded by cataracts.

## ABOUT ART HISTORY

Monet made a large contribution to the development of Impressionism through his ideas and painting. Unlike most painters before him, Monet painted outdoors. He made careful observations of subject matter, studying the changes in appearance due to light and weather. In the first Impressionist exhibition, Monet included a work titled *Impression, Sunrise.* A critic, ridiculing the colors, strange distortion of shapes, and loose brush strokes, derived the name *Impressionism* from this title. The term *Impressionism* was soon accepted and used by the public to describe this new style of painting.

## ABOUT THE ARTWORK

Monet painted landscapes and people, but he especially loved scenes that included water. At one time, he had a floating studio: he filled a rowboat with art supplies and painted in the

*Archive Photos*

shade of a striped awning. Toward the end of his life, Monet painted huge landscapes of the garden and lily ponds near his home in Giverny, France.

## ABOUT THE MEDIA

Although he made sketches later in life, Monet created mostly oil paintings. By the 1870s, Monet eliminated black from his palette, replacing it with blue.

## ABOUT THE TECHNIQUE

Monet often began a painting by covering the canvas with a background color. Then, he dabbed paint here and there until shapes became recognizable. He was fascinated by the way the same color could look different at certain times of the day or during particular weather conditions. He often painted the same subjects over and over again to capture this in his paintings. Examples of motifs he painted many times include Rouen Cathedral, poplars, haystacks, and water lilies.

# Louise Nevelson (lū ēz´ nev´ əl sən)
## (1900–1988)

## About the Artist

Nevelson was born in Russia. She moved to Maine with her family when she was five. Later she studied art in New York City and in Germany. Besides being interested in sculpture, Nevelson was also interested in drawing, painting, singing, and acting. In 1932, Nevelson helped Diego Rivera create a huge mural in New York. By 1941, she had her first show. None of her realistic sculptures in the show sold, so she destroyed them all! When Nevelson started making sculpture assembled from discarded materials, people finally saw her talent. Her metal sculptures *Shadows and Flags* are in a square in New York City. In 1978, the square was renamed the Louise Nevelson Plaza.

### ABOUT ART HISTORY

Nevelson was a leader in the field of modern sculpture. She was one of the first to create room-sized sculptures. She was also one of the first to put "found objects," into her sculpture. Found objects are things like broken pieces of furniture, old tools, baseball bats, and wood trim from houses.

### ABOUT THE ARTWORK

Nevelson is famous for her huge nonobjective, assembled sculptures. These have been called "sculptural landscapes." One type is made of open wooden boxes stacked to form walls. The boxes are like the rows of glass jars in a candy store from her childhood. Inside each box, Nevelson put pieces of wood and other materials. She usually sprayed a whole creation one color, often black, white, or gold.

*Al Mozell/Photo Researchers*

### ABOUT THE MEDIA

Nevelson made her first sculptures out of wood. Later she used black steel, Plexiglas, Lucite, and other materials. She also created lithographs and collages.

### ABOUT THE TECHNIQUE

This artist unified the different forms of wood in her work by painting them a single color. First, she used black, then white and gold. Her plastic and metal pieces are unpainted.

## About the Artist

Noland was born in North Carolina. He is a well-known American abstract painter. His father was an amateur painter. Using his father's art supplies, Noland began to paint when he was only eight or nine. He served as a glider pilot during World War II. Later he studied art and music at college. He became an art teacher. He had his first one-person exhibition in Paris in 1949 when he was 25. Noland married twice and has three children.

### ABOUT ART HISTORY

Noland builds upon the minimalist work of Josef Albers. He experimented with Abstract Expressionism. About 1958, he began painting circles inside each other. He is well-known for this style of painting. The simple look of circle art was a big change from the detailed abstract paintings that had been popular.

### ABOUT THE ARTWORK

Noland began by painting geometric shapes. Later, he focused on circles. Then, he painted chevrons (v-shaped patterns), diamonds, and stripes. He has also cut his finished canvases into different shapes. Noland is always searching for ways to show his ideas with color.

*Chris Felver/Archive Photos*

### ABOUT THE MEDIA

Noland works primarily with thinned acrylic paint, applying it directly to raw canvas. He is known for his unusual diamond-shaped and elongated rectangular canvases.

### ABOUT THE TECHNIQUE

For large circle paintings, Noland staples the canvas to the floor. Sometimes he paints directly on it. Other times he starts by mixing forty or so jars of Magna. Then he draws rings of color on paper to see how the colors work together. Sometimes he traces around dinner plates with a pencil to draw the rings. Then he paints the rings, beginning with the center circle and working out to the edges. Noland chooses his final colors as he paints.

# Georgia O'Keeffe (jôr´ jə ō kēf´)
### *(1887–1986)*

## About the Artist

O'Keeffe was born in Sun Prairie, Wisconsin. At the age of 10, she began taking private art lessons. But the thing she liked most was experimenting with art at home. By the age of 13, she had decided to become an artist. She trained under experts and won many prizes for her art.

For years, she challenged the art world with her unique vision. She eventually became famous for her spectacular, larger-than-life paintings of such natural objects as flowers, animal skulls, and shells. She loved nature, especially the desert of New Mexico, where she spent the last half of her life. O'Keeffe was married to the famous American photographer Alfred Stieglitz and appears in many of his photographs.

On June 17, 1997, a Georgia O'Keeffe Museum opened in Santa Fe, New Mexico. This is the first museum in the United States devoted exclusively to the work of a major women artist.

## ABOUT THE ART HISTORY

The photographer Alfred Stieglitz promoted modern artists and photographers from Europe and America through a magazine called *Camera Work* and a gallery known as "291." O'Keeffe and the circle of artists she met through Stieglitz were pioneers of modernism in the United States. She took subjects into her imagination and altered and simplified their appearance. She expressed her emotions through her vivid paintings.

## ABOUT THE ARTWORK

O'Keeffe's artwork features bold, colorful, abstract patterns and shapes. O'Keeffe most

*UPI/Corbis-Bettmann*

often painted such natural forms as flowers and bleached bones, leaving out their normal backgrounds. She never painted people, but sometimes painted landscapes.

## ABOUT THE MEDIA

O'Keeffe used oil paints and watercolors for her paintings. She used pastels, charcoal, and pencil for her drawings.

## ABOUT THE TECHNIQUE

O'Keeffe used dazzling, jewel-toned colors. She chose unusual perspectives, such as very close up or far away. She also enlarged the scale of her subjects.

# Harriet Powers (hâr´ ē ət  pou´ ərz)
## (1837–1911)

## About the Artist

Powers was born a slave in Athens, Georgia. When she was freed, she and her husband bought a small farm where they raised their children. Powers raised chickens, worked as a seamstress, and made patchwork quilts until she died in 1911. Although she did not gain fame as a quilt artist in her lifetime, her exquisite quilts now hang in the Smithsonian Institute.

### ABOUT ART HISTORY
Although quilting is a European art form, a uniquely African artistry showed through in the quilts made by slaves. Today African American quilts are a record of cultural survival.

### ABOUT THE ART WORK
Powers is known to have sewn at least two quilts between 1886 and 1898. The pictures on the quilts tell stories of the Bible.

*Courtesy, Museum of Fine Arts, Boston*

### ABOUT THE MEDIA
Powers used fabric scraps and thread to complete her quilts. Some decorative metallic thread was used to highlight detail in the quilt.

### ABOUT THE TECHNIQUE
The quilts of Harriet Powers have been tied to African textile origins. Her figures are very simple and minimal. They were usually cut from the same piece of cloth. She created images that were universal symbols.

# Rembrandt van Rijn (rem´ bränt vän rīn´)
## (1606–1669)

## About the Artist

Rembrandt Harmenszoon van Rijn was the most influential Dutch artist of the seventeenth century. The seventh of nine children born to a miller, Rembrandt showed talent early in life. His parents took great interest in providing him education despite their modest income. Rembrandt studied a short time at the Leiden Latin School to prepare for a profession as a city administrator. His parents eventually removed him from school and placed him in apprenticeships with painters. After moving to Amsterdam in 1631, he gained the commissions of several wealthy patrons and achieved much success. Rembrandt spent a large portion of the money he earned at auctions and on collecting. Though his financial and personal life was turbulent, he continued to produce works of art until his death in 1669.

### ABOUT ART HISTORY

Most painters during the 1600s traveled to Italy to study art. Italian art and artists such as Michelangelo and Raphael were highly esteemed at this time. Rembrandt, however, chose to remain in Holland to learn about art. His remarkable ability to show feeling and emotions through dramatic lighting has made his work universally understandable and appreciated. Rembrandt is considered to be one of the greatest western artists from all periods and countries.

*Sid Richardson Collection Of Western Art*

### ABOUT THE ARTWORK

Under the painter Pieter Lastman, Rembrandt learned how to create dramatic accents through the means of light and shadow, gestures, expression and composition. In all,

Rembrandt created well over 600 paintings as well as a large number of drawings, etchings, and more than 60 self-portraits. The subjects of his works were largely portraits, but he also painted historical, biblical, and mythological subjects.

### ABOUT THE MEDIA

Rembrandt worked mainly in oils on wood and canvas. He completed many drawings on paper with pen and ink and also created several etchings.

### ABOUT THE TECHNIQUE

Rembrandt used a technique called *chiaroscuro*, an Italian word meaning "light and dark." He used light to focus attention on certain areas that contained the details. He left other parts in shadows using dark colors.

# Sir James J. Shannon (jāmz shan´ən)
## *(1862–1923)*

## About the Artist

Known as J.J., James Jebusa Shannon was born in New York of Irish parents. Even as a boy, he showed talent for drawing and was sent to England in 1878 to study at the Royal College of Art. Several of his instructors at the college were French artists. A promising student, Shannon was asked to paint a portrait of a woman on the queen's staff. This picture marked the beginning of his career as a portrait painter.

Shannon married in 1886 and had a daughter the next year. He painted his wife and daughter many times. As more and more wealthy people asked him to paint them, he became wealthy himself. He traveled to Europe and throughout the United States. His paintings were shown all around the world.

In 1912, Shannon was injured in a riding accident and afterward slowly lost the use of his legs. Around the same time, his style of portrait painting became less popular as the modern art movement took over. He died in 1923.

### ABOUT ART HISTORY

Artist James Whistler once insisted that Shannon resign his membership in the Royal Academy of Art because its artists had become "too commercial." Shannon made a good living painting portraits. He did not resign.

### ABOUT THE ARTWORK

Shannon painted portraits of the wealthy, of ordinary people, and of his own family. He wanted to create not just a picture that looked like his subject, but an image of beauty.

### ABOUT THE MEDIA

This artist painted his subjects in oils on canvas.

*National Museum of American Art, Washington DC/Art Resource, NY*

### ABOUT THE TECHNIQUE

Shannon's work showed the influence of his French instructors, but his style varied from painting to painting. Some of this was due to his own experimentation, but at times he had to adjust his style to please the person he was painting. His work was sometimes light and impressionistic; other times, it was dark and realistic. Some of his best paintings were those of his wife and daughter.

## About the Artist

Steichen was born in Luxembourg and emigrated to the United States with his family when he was still a child. Steichen initially trained as a painter and took up photography to aid in making drawings for a lithographic firm. Steichen met the photographer Alfred Stieglitz while passing through New York en route to Paris. Stieglitz not only purchased many of Steichen's photographs, but also encouraged him to continue experimenting with the camera. During World War I, Steichen was chief of the photographic division of the army air corps, and in World War II he directed a U.S. navy combat photography team. Steichen is also well-known for his photographs of noteworthy personalities such as Auguste Rodin, Charlie Chaplin, and Greta Garbo. In 1947, Steichen was appointed director of photography for the Museum of Modern Art in New York.

### ABOUT ART HISTORY

In 1902, Steichen joined Alfred Stieglitz in the founding of the Photo-Secession, an organization dedicated to promoting photography as a fine art. In 1955, Steichen curated a photographic exhibit called "The Family of Man" for the Museum of Modern Art. The 503 photographs, compiled from amateur and professional photographers, focused on the real-life subject of human solidarity, and became the most influential exhibition of photography at the time.

### ABOUT THE ARTWORK

Steichen's own photographs initially gained fame for their resemblance to paintings. During World War I, Steichen aimed for maximum realism. It was at this time that he

*Wayne Miller/Magnum Photos*

began to develop photography as a modern art form that could capture everyday life.

### ABOUT THE MEDIA

Steichen's medium is photography.

### ABOUT THE TECHNIQUE

In Steichen's earlier work, he frequently brushed on silver salts or other chemicals to negatives or paper in order to achieve soft, fuzzy pictures. Sometimes to create a blurry image he would kick his tripod. These misty pictures were considered by most critics of his day to be the highest achievement of photographic art. As his career progressed, he aimed to create photographs with maximum detail, definition, and brilliance.

# Monika Steinhoff (mon´ē kä stīn´hof)
## (1942-    )

## About the Artist

Steinhoff was born in Germany. When she was five years old, her family moved to a military base in Alamogordo, New Mexico. The beauty of the landscape had a strong effect on her. She decided that she wanted to become an artist so she could recreate that beauty. She went to art school but lacked confidence and switched her major to English. While working on her doctorate in literature, she decided to start experimenting with art again. She taught herself how to do watercolors, batik, and sculpture. Now, she is well-known for her brightly colored interior and street scenes of New Mexico.

### ABOUT ART HISTORY
Steinhoff says she has been influenced by many artists, including Milton Avery, Frida Kahlo, Paul Klee, Henri Matisse, George Tooker, and Henri de Toulouse-Latrec.

### ABOUT THE ARTWORK
Steinhoff usually paints interior scenes of Santa Fe, New Mexico. She recreates hangouts and the patrons who frequent them. She is fascinated by how people interact with one another. Most of the characters in her paintings are based on real people she has met in Santa Fe. Hotel and restaurant owners often commission Steinhoff to paint scenes from their establishments. Steinhoff has also painted a series of street scenes. Her paintings are bright, colorful, and realistic.

*Photo by Sean O'Friel*

### ABOUT THE MEDIA
Steinhoff has worked in many media. When she decided to become an artist, she made batiks, using wax and dye on cloth. Currently, she devotes herself to painting with oils on linen and silk. She also makes etchings with *aquatint,* a process that produces the tones of watercolors.

### ABOUT THE TECHNIQUE
Steinhoff applies layer after layer of paint to create a richness on the surface of her canvases. She makes her paintings look realistic through her use of color. In her interior scenes, she uses a high point of view. For her landscapes, she prefers a low point of view and sometimes exaggerates perspectives.

# Joseph Stella (jō′ zef stel′ ə)
## (1877–1946)

## About the Artist

Stella was born in Italy. He came to the United States as a young man and began painting portraits of immigrants living in New York City. A group concerned about immigrants was impressed with Stella's work. The group sent him to the coal mines and industrial regions of Pennsylvania and West Virginia. Stella painted the workers there so that others would understand the terrible working conditions they faced. Stella saw how the growth of industry and the use of machines was affecting human lives. However, he was also impressed by the power and creativity of the American industrial age. In time, he turned from painting the workers to painting symbolic pictures of technology and machines.

*©1943 Arnold Newman*

### ABOUT ART HISTORY

Stella was one of the first artists to combine European abstract painting techniques with modern American subjects. Following the abstract style, Stella did not try to show realistic details. Instead, he represented what he saw with a combination of forms, colors, lines, and surfaces.

### ABOUT THE ARTWORK

Stella painted the Brooklyn Bridge several times because he felt its lines and angles represented the energy and opportunity of New York City. His pictures of the bridge have been used on posters and in textbooks and exhibitions to symbolize the city. In fact, people are so fascinated by these pictures that they tend to overlook Stella's later work. In his later life, he returned to his Italian background and more traditional painting styles. He then created impressive landscapes, portraits, religious images, and still lifes.

### ABOUT THE MEDIA

This artist mainly created oil paintings.

### ABOUT THE TECHNIQUE

Stella combined several points of view in the same picture. He used vivid, glowing colors and geometric patterns.

# Gilbert Stuart (gil´ bûrt  stu´ ərt)
## (1755–1828)

## About the Artist

Stuart was born in Rhode Island. A Scottish painter named Cosmo Alexander recognized the 14-year-old boy's artistic talent. In 1771, Alexander took Stuart to Scotland to study painting but died soon afterward. Stuart took a job as a sailor so he could return to Rhode Island. There, he began painting portraits of Newport families. However, when the Revolutionary War began, Stuart sailed off to London. The popular portrait style in Britain at that time was much more ornate than Stuart's simple approach, so he had few customers. He went to work for Benjamin West, another American in England and the King's painter. With West's guidance, Stuart began to paint in a more decorative style. After his painting *The Skater* won widespread recognition in 1782, he had many customers. In 1787, he moved to Ireland, where people begged him to paint them. Unfortunately, Stuart spent money even faster than he earned it. In 1793, he returned to the United States to escape his debts and continue his career.

## ABOUT ART HISTORY
After working with Benjamin West, Stuart turned from a simple, tightly controlled painting style to one that was more complex, sophisticated, and flowing. Stuart was also influenced by English portrait paintings of Thomas Gainsborough and Sir Joshua Reynold, who painted during the same period.

## ABOUT THE ARTWORK
This artist is famous for his portraits of George Washington, which can often be seen in textbooks and on posters and stamps. Stuart also painted other famous men and women of that time–

*Culver Pictures*

Thomas Jefferson, James Madison, John Adams, King George III, and King George IV. His portraits, which number nearly one thousand, have brought him lasting fame.

## ABOUT THE MEDIA
Stuart worked mainly in oils on canvas.

## ABOUT THE TECHNIQUE
Stuart did not sketch before he began painting. He thought sketching was a waste of time. Stuart often tried to amuse his subjects with stories as he painted them. That way, he thought their portraits would look more lifelike and perhaps include a smile.

**30**

# Roxanne Swentzell (rokz´ an  swent´ zəl)
## (1962-     )

## About the Artist

Swentzell was born in Taos, New Mexico, in 1962. She is half Santa Clara Pueblo Indian. When she was a little girl, she sat and watched her mother make pots out of the earth surrounding their home. Swentzell liked to shape clay into figures. She had a hard time talking to other people and tried to express her feelings through the little people she made out of clay. Her family saw that she was very talented. As a teenager, she attended the Institute of American Indian Arts and the Portland Museum Art School. She went to college at the Pacific Northwest College of Art. She currently works and lives in Santa Clara, New Mexico.

## ABOUT ART HISTORY

This Santa Clara Pueblo family spans five generations of potters, sculptors, architects, and teachers. There are many Native American artists who no longer make traditional Native American art like beadwork and pottery. They are trying to break the sterotypical images of Native Americans. Swentzell and other artists make art that shows they are trying to balance a twentieth-century mainstream life with a respect for the traditions of Santa Clara Pueblo culture.

## ABOUT THE ARTWORK

Swentzell makes large, hollow figurines that reflect Santa Clara Pueblo stories, her life, and the lives of those around her. She explores the emotional side of people through her art.

*Roxanne Swentzell*

Through the body positions, hand gestures, and facial expressions in her figures, Swentzell communicates universal feelings. Each sculpture is one color and void of decoration. Her figures are large, but are restricted to the size of her kiln.

## ABOUT THE MEDIA

Swentzell uses clay indiginous to her area of the United States to create her ceramic sculpture.

## ABOUT THE TECHNIQUE

Swentzell uses a coil technique to make her sculptures. She forms a hollow body, then adds arms and legs. To make a face, she uses her fingers and her knife to sculpt the clay. She polishes the surface with her knife. She dries the sculpture for several weeks before firing it in a kiln.

# Tom Thomson (tom  tom´ sən)
## (1877–1917)

## About the Artist

Thomson was born in Claremont, Ontario, Canada, to a Scottish family. He was a quiet, modest man who lived a simple life. He began his art career by working as a commercial artist. He was very interested in Canada's Far North. At the age of 35, he decided to try to paint it. He quit his job. In only three and half years, Thomson finished nearly 300 sketches and two dozen oil paintings. At first, not many people thought his artwork was good. Lumberjacks and trappers who knew the Far North were among the few who did. Thomson did not have much money. However, after his death, his paintings became popular. Now they hang in many Canadian galleries. Small sketches that he couldn't sell for $25 have sold for more than $5,000. Thomson, an expert canoeist, drowned in 1917 in the lake he loved to paint. He was only 40. The shack where he lived alone and painted has been restored as a museum.

## ABOUT ART HISTORY

At a time when few Canadians were painting, Thomson was one of the Group of Seven. This Canadian group helped promote the country's artists, landscape, and people. Thomson helped other Canadian artists create their own styles. He let them know they did not need to copy European painting techniques. His style is known as Regionalism.

## ABOUT THE ARTWORK

Thomson mainly painted a region called Algonquin Park in Ontario.

*McMichael Canadian Art Collection Archives*

He worked from early spring until the November snows, painting the wildlife, lumber camps, and landscape. He painted few people.

## ABOUT THE MEDIA

Thomson worked mostly in oils on canvas.

## ABOUT THE TECHNIQUE

Thomson's early work as a commercial artist helped him master the techniques of painting. He painted directly from nature and used rich colors.

# Vincent van Gogh (vin sent´ van gō´)
## *(1853 – 1890)*

## About the Artist

Even as a boy in Holland, van Gogh cared about other people very much. He tried many jobs, including being a teacher, minister, and social worker. However, he had problems getting along with nearly everyone except his younger brother, Theo. At the age of 28, van Gogh decided that the best way he could serve others was through art. He expressed his deep feelings about people through his paintings. As he moved from place to place, he left many of his works behind. Some were burned in fireplaces for heat or even used to patch holes in walls. Van Gogh was quite poor his entire life and often went hungry so that he could buy painting supplies. Van Gogh died at age 37.

### ABOUT ART HISTORY
Even though van Gogh sold only one painting in his lifetime, today he is considered the greatest nineteenth century Dutch artist. He was one of the first to express his feelings through painting. This new school of art is now called Expressionism.

### ABOUT THE ARTWORK
Van Gogh painted many different subjects, from portraits to landscapes. He once lived in France near fields of golden wheat and sunflowers, which he painted many times. He wrote that his sunflowers symbolized his gratitude toward others, especially his brother, one of the few people who encouraged him to paint.

Self Portrait with Straw Hat

### ABOUT THE MEDIA
During the ten short years that van Gogh worked, he created hundreds of oil paintings, along with many drawings in ink, crayon, chalk, and charcoal.

### ABOUT THE TECHNIQUE
Van Gogh wanted to show energy and motion in his work. He often put complementary colors, such as red and green, next to each other to add power to his paintings. He applied oil paints in thick layers, sometimes straight from the tubes. His thick layers, slashing brush strokes, and swirling shapes gave his paintings strong patterns that reflected his strong feelings.

# Max Weber (maks web´ər)
## (1881–1961)

## About the Artist

Weber was born in a region of Russia that is now Poland. In 1891, his family emigrated to New York City. Weber studied art at the Pratt Institute in Brooklyn, NY. He also studied in Paris and spent several months traveling through Europe. He returned to the United States to paint and write articles about art and color for *Camera Work,* a journal published by Alfred Stieglitz. In 1911, Stieglitz arranged an exhibition for Weber's work. Weber married in 1916. He taught art to support his wife and two children because as his paintings were not selling. By his 1930 exhibition at New York's Museum of Modern Art, the art world was beginning to appreciate his work. Toward the end of his life, he focused mainly on sculpture. Throughout his career, Weber wrote poetry and essays about art.

### ABOUT ART HISTORY

Weber, a leader of the modern art movement in the United States, was greatly influenced by Paul Cézanne. Weber was friends with Rousseau and Matisse and admired the work of Picasso and Kandinsky.

### ABOUT THE ARTWORK

In the painting *Chinese Restaurant,* Weber painted motifs of tabletops, floor tiling, and wood paneling in a cubist style. The subject was inspired by a visit to a Chinese restaurant, then still a novelty in America. Weber's work includes portraits, landscapes, and still lifes. After World War I, Weber focused more on his Jewish heritage.

*Archive Photos*

He also experimented with nonobjective sculpture.

### ABOUT THE MEDIA

In addition to oil paintings, Weber created small sculptures, prints, watercolors, drawings, and woodcuts.

### ABOUT THE TECHNIQUE

In his early cubist paintings, Weber suggested figures with flattened spaces and blocks of bright color. He fragmented the motifs extracted from the *Chinese Restaurant,* placing them in a distinctly cubist arrangement. In the 1930s, Weber used line more actively. In the 1950s, he reintroduced cubist distortion into his work.

# Jane Wilson (jān wil´ sən)
## (1924-     )

## About the Artist

Wilson was born and grew up in Iowa. That state's wide-open landscapes are evident in many of her paintings. She also paints shore scenes. Wilson earned college degrees in art history and painting. When she married, she moved to New York City, where her husband grew up. To help pay their bills, Wilson worked as a model for seven years. She painted at night and on weekends. In 1960, the Museum of Modern Art bought one of her paintings and her art career took off. She has a daughter and has taught art at many colleges across the nation.

*Oscar White/Corbis*

## ABOUT ART HISTORY

Wilson's art style is hard to classify. Like the Impressionists, she is interested in light. However, some objects in her still lifes seem abstract. Her still lifes focus on the surfaces of objects. Her landscapes focus on the play of light and weather. She says she paints scenes as they appear to her, not necessarily as they are.

## ABOUT THE ARTWORK

Wilson paints still lifes, landscapes, and shorescapes. One of her paintings, *Sun After Rain,* shows sunlight filtering through gathering clouds. *Winter Tea Time* is a collection of pitchers and pots painted in a beige and gray "winter light."

## ABOUT THE MEDIA

This artist generally works in oils on canvas.

## ABOUT THE TECHNIQUE

Wilson does not sketch her ideas. Sometimes she photographs a scene she plans to paint. She starts landscapes with the sky. As the paint dries, she chooses a place for the horizon. She often places the horizon low in the painting. Then she paints with stabbing motions. This makes thin layers of color for a hazy look. One painting might have 30 layers of paint on it. The colors are usually warm neutrals, browns, and soft yellows. Sometimes she scrapes away layers of paint to show the colors underneath.

# Frank Lloyd Wright (frangk loid rīt)
## (1867–1959)

## About the Artist

Wright was born in Richland Center, Wisconsin. His father left when he was 16. His mother wanted him to be an architect. As a young boy, he and his mother arranged blocks, paper, and other simple materials into shapes of buildings and furniture. Wright studied engineering at the University of Wisconsin for less than two years before moving to Chicago. He eventually found a job at the architectural firm of Adler and Sullivan where he worked with the important modern architect Louis Henri Sullivan for five years. In 1893, Wright began his own practice. He traveled in Europe and then lived in Japan between 1915 and 1922, during the construction of the Imperial Hotel in Tokyo that he designed. In 1928, he declared personal and professional bankruptcy and, as a result, all of his possessions were sold. During the Great Depression of the 1930s, Wright designed several buildings, but none were constructed. He supported himself by lecturing and writing. After the end of World War II, Wright received many commissions. By the end of his career, he had designed more than 400 buildings.

## ABOUT ART HISTORY

Wright is known as a modern architect. His mentor Louis Henri Sullivan is known as the first modern architect. Sullivan's architectural philosophy was "form follows function." This means that the architectural design of a building should follow from the use of the building. This was a radical idea at the end of the 20th century.

## ABOUT THE MEDIA

Under the influence of Sullivan, Wright developed what became known as the "Prairie Style." Open interiors and long, low exteriors, with hipped roofs and wide overhangs characterize

*Ralph Crane/Black Star*

this architecture. During the 1930s, he designed a style of house called the "Usonian." These were small, modular houses. In 1943, he designed the Guggenheim Museum in New York City.

## ABOUT THE TECHNIQUE

Wright experimented with materials when he designed buildings. He custom-designed concrete blocks for some houses. He also designed houses with modern features, including concrete slab floors that incorporated pipes for hot-water heating and wood with sandwich walls assembled on the building site.

# Peggy Flora Zalucha (peg´ ē flôr´ ə zə lū´ chə)
## (1948–    )

## About the Artist

Zalucha was born in Peoria, Illinois. She was raised to appreciate photography and encouraged to take pictures of the world around her. When Zalucha was in college, women were not advised to get studio degrees. So Zalucha got her degree in teaching instead. Her first official job was as an art teacher in a rural Nebraska school. Zalucha has been making and teaching art for over twenty years.

*Courtesy Peggy Flora Zalucha*

## ABOUT ART HISTORY

Zalucha's paintings have been classified as modern examples of genre painting. Genre painting is the art of finding beauty in everyday life. Many of Zalucha's subjects are incorporated into traditional still-life painting styles.

## ABOUT THE ARTWORK

Zalucha's paintings are a celebration of daily life. She thinks that there is much beauty in these common things that we often overlook. By using water color paints, Zalucha feels she can unleash the jewel-like quality of her still life paintings.

## ABOUT THE MEDIA

Zalucha primarily chooses to use watercolor paints on paper. She also uses acrylic washes and India ink from time to time.

## ABOUT THE TECHNIQUE

Zalucha feels that when she comes across new problems in her artwork, she is able to learn from her own paintings. Watercolor is a difficult medium to rework because it can't be painted over. Zalucha feels that she has come upon her own style using this medium. She uses the watercolor paints to allow the object she is painting to shimmer and shine. This uncovers the magic of the object so that it is no longer ordinary.

## About the Artist

Öndür Gegen or Zanabazar, was a Mongolian leader during the seventeenth and eighteenth centuries. His long and productive career as a politician, Buddhist lama, and artist influenced a cultural movement that swept over Mongolia, Tibet, and China. Zanabazar had a noble background as a direct descendent of several rulers. He was first and foremost a truly devout Buddhist monk, who spent years in serious study and retreat as a young man. He became a theologian and scholar, a linguist, an architect, a sculptor, and a painter. Within a century after his death, Zanabazar had a mythical reputation, which probably emerged from being a multitalented genius in real life.

### ABOUT ART HISTORY

Most Mongols lived a nomadic life and moved their homes from place to place according to the changes in seasons. The nomadic life had an impact on the art of Mongolia, because it limited works to items that could easily be transported. Therefore, most artistic expression is found in the ornamentation of useful objects like clothing, saddles, and utensils. Most of the monasteries in Khalkha, or Outer Mongolia where Zanabazar lived, were seminomadic. The permanent temples built were designed in a Chinese or Tibetan style and decorated with religious ceremonial objects. Monks, like other Mongols, lived in round tents called *yurts*.

### ABOUT THE ARTWORK

While living a traditional, nomadic monk life,

*Zanabazar. (Mongolian).* Buddha.

Zanabazar learned the art of bronze casting from Nepalese artists working in Tibetan monasteries. He began making his own sophisticated works of art, all intended for use in Buddhist ritual. Some of these works were statues of Buddha, the central enlightened figure of Buddhism. This Buddha is considered to be created by the school of Zanabazar, but cannot be directly attributed to the artist.

### ABOUT THE MEDIA

This Buddha is made of gilt bronze. Precious jewels were sometimes inlaid for decoration.

### ABOUT THE TECHNIQUE

This artist cast bronze into molds to create his statues. This Buddha image was also gilded in gold.

# Indonesian Shadow Puppet

## About the Artist

Indonesia is a country in Southeast Asia that consists of more than 13,600 islands. The islands lie along the equator and extend more than 3,000 miles, ranking Indonesia fifth in population among all countries. The most famous arts of Indonesia include dances of the old royal courts of Java and the dramatic folk dances of Bali. Puppet dramas are a major part of Javanese and Balinese culture. The most popular puppets are flat and made of leather.

### ABOUT ART HISTORY

Shadow theater is part of the general development of theater in Southeast Asia. The first theater consisted of characters drawn on long sheets of paper. The dalang unrolled the paper as he told the story. During the fifteenth century, shadow theater became children's entertainment. About that time, the moving shadow puppets were developed to tell religious stories. More recent theater uses masked human actors in place of puppets. The audience watches the actors, not their shadows.

*Artist Unknown. (Indonesia).* Indonesian Shadow Puppet. *c. 1950. Cut, painted leather. 31½ inches high. Private Collection.*

### ABOUT THE MEDIA

Some early shadow puppets were made from thin wood or buffalo skin carved into intricate designs. In time, rounded puppets that looked more like humans became popular. These puppets wore elaborately carved, painted, or printed costumes. The shadow puppets were either princes, sages (wise men), apes, officers, or clowns.

### ABOUT THE TECHNIQUE

One type of shadow theater takes place outside. Shadows from the puppets are projected onto a long screen. The light is often a flickering oil lamp. The dalang sits in front of the screen, in view of the men in the audience. The women sit on the other side of the screen and watch the shadows. Musicians accompany the story, which may last more than one night.

### ABOUT THE ARTWORK

One example of shadow theater is "The Story of Arayana," a story of love and revenge among the ancient rajahs.

# The Pyramids at Giza

## About the Artist

The Pyramids at Giza were built as tombs for the Pharaoh Cheops, his son Chephren, and his grandson Mycenius. Smaller pyramids for family members surround the tomb of Mycenius. The most famous of the pyramids is known as "The Great Pyramid." It housed the body of Cheops. The laborers who worked on the pyramids are unknown. The inside of each tomb was decorated with sculptures, wall paintings, and carvings to accompany the pharaoh's *ka* (spirit) into the afterworld. The bodies of all three pharaohs, as well as the treasures they were buried with, disappeared from the tombs long ago.

## ABOUT ART HISTORY

Pyramid building is distinctively Egyptian. The forerunners of the Pyramids at Giza include the Step Pyramid of Zoser, and the two pyramids built for Snofru at Dahshur. The Step Pyramid of Zoser was designed by an Egyptian named Imhotep. He was the first Egyptian to build with stone instead of brick. Before pharaohs were buried in pyramids, they were buried in oblong brick structures called *mastabas.*

## ABOUT THE ARTWORK

The Pyramids at Giza were listed as one of the Seven Wonders of the World by the Greeks in the second century B.C. They are the only Wonder that stands today. Egyptians believed that the deceased—especially pharaohs—needed a house that could last

*Artist unknown. (Egypt).* The Pyramids at Giza. *(c. 2470 B.C.), Chefren (c. 2500 B.C.), and Cheops (c. 2530 B.C.). Giza.* © *Fred J. Maroon/Photo Researchers, Inc.*

forever. The inside of each tomb was decorated with everything that the pharaoh's *ka* could need. There were imitation doors made of stone or plaster that the pharaoh's *ka* could pass through.

## ABOUT THE MEDIA

The pyramids were made from blocks of limestone, wood, and mortar.

## ABOUT THE TECHNIQUE

Most scientists believe that the Nile River sometimes flooded the valley where Giza sits, near Cairo, Egypt. When the valley was flooded, the stones (which weigh about two and a half tons in the Great Pyramid alone) could be moved in boats. The Greek historian Herodotus estimated that the pyramids were built by groups of about 100,000 men who worked in three-month shifts.

# The Great Sphinx

## About the Artist

The Great Sphinx stands at Giza between the pyramidal tombs of Chephren and Cheops. It is shaped like a lion, with the idealized face of Chephren, a pleated headdress, a cobra (or uraeus), and an Osiris beard. It is a mixture of king, god, and lion. It was carved from a natural limestone projection. Like the pyramids, the Great Sphinx was carved by the hands of many Egyptians.

## ABOUT ART HISTORY

The Sphinx first appeared in Ancient Egyptian culture as both an animal revered for its power and a beast that represented the pharaoh king. The lion could represent the presence of a god. It was also found in the image of Tefnut, the goddess of rain and dew who had a lion's head. Most sphinxes were male. There is a female sphinx at Abu Roash, the tomb of Chephren's half-brother. The sphinx image also appears in Greek culture, but much differently. Greek sphinxes are angry, have wings, and are usually female.

*The Great Sphinx*

have to move the giant piece of limestone. It may also be true that the piece of limestone looked like a lion before it was carved into the image of the Sphinx. For centuries, the Sphinx was covered with drifted sand. For a time, people believed it was a construction of the gods. The remains of a Sphinx Temple show that the Sphinx itself was thought of as a god. In 1997, it was restored to repair its wind-damaged surface.

## ABOUT THE ARTWORK

The Great Sphinx is carved from a natural protrusion of limestone. It represents the image of the king of Upper and Lower Egypt, part man and part lion. The Sphinx sits with its paws outstretched. Some scientists believe that it was carved so that workers would not

## ABOUT THE MEDIA

The Sphinx is carved from limestone.

## ABOUT THE TECHNIQUE

The Sphinx was carved by a group of skilled workers. Like the pyramids, the work must have taken an immense amount of cooperation. It is a great example of the advanced building methods and detailed organization of ancient Egyptian culture.

# Pantheon

## About the Artist

Although the architect is unknown, the Roman Emperor Hadrian was responsible for the building and restoration of many Roman structures during his rule (A.D. 117–A.D. 138). The decision to build the Pantheon, a temple to all the Roman gods, was part of Hadrian's plan to build a safe and self-sufficient city. Agrippa's ancient Pantheon of 27 B.C. was replaced with the Pantheon that stands today. Bridges, roads, public baths, and monuments were also built during Hadrian's rule, illustrating his beliefs that Rome should be self-sufficient and prosperous.

### ABOUT ART HISTORY

The Pantheon was one of the most important pieces of architecture of all time. It showed the full potential of concrete as a building material as well as a way to define architectural space. Many buildings since have copied its design and structure.

*Artist unknown. (Italy).* Pantheon. *A.D. 118–128. Concrete, brick, marble, and bronze. 141 feet high. Rome, Italy. Photographer: Louis Grandadam/© Tony Stone Images.*

hides the vast rotunda. This porch has 16 granite columns that divide the porch into three aisles. The central aisle leads to the main door. Each of the two side aisles leads to an apse (rounded hollow) where statues of two Roman emperors, Augustus and Agrippa, stood.

### ABOUT THE ARTWORK

The Pantheon is a Roman temple built in honor of the Roman gods. It was begun around A.D. 118 and finished in 125. Unlike Christian churches, the Pantheon was not built for people to gather in. It stands as a monument of quiet peace to the gods. The only source of light in the Pantheon comes from a window at the top of its great rotunda. The diameter and height of the rotunda are the same—43.2 meters. The front of the building has a columned porch that

### ABOUT THE MEDIA

The Pantheon is constructed of granite, concrete, marble, stone, bronze, brick, mortar, lead, and very little wood.

### ABOUT THE TECHNIQUE

The dome was made of concrete, shaped entirely by a wood structure. A complex system of arches in the hall and the lower part of the rotunda allowed workers to build on different levels of the building at the same time.

# Self-Portrait Mask

## About the Artist

The Haida are Native Americans who live on the Queen Charlotte Islands off the coast of British Columbia. Supporting themselves by fishing and hunting, the Haida are well-known for their woodworking skills. Out of the red cedar of the surrounding rain forest, they carve canoes, boxes, masks, and totem poles that record family histories. They also document their beliefs and traditional myths in wood. In the past, only men were permitted to become carvers. Boys who showed early skill in working with wood were trained to become specialists. Early Haida artists did not sign their work, so it is impossible to identify the most skilled among them.

### ABOUT ART HISTORY

Haida carving techniques and symbolism are handed down from generation to generation.

### ABOUT THE ARTWORK

The Haida use flowing, curving lines to form nostrils, eyes, and lips on their masks. Many of the lines run parallel and then taper to a point. Only small areas are left as flat, empty spaces on the masks. The craftsmen add small amounts of red and black paint as decoration. Masks, other than self-portraits, often represent mythical beings or animals, such as the wolf, bear, beaver, or a sea creature. Many of these masks are worn during four-day ceremonies and then buried.

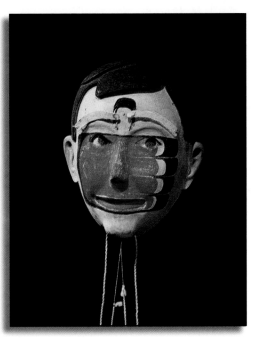

*Haida. (North American).* Self-Portrait Mask. *Pre-1900. Carved wood, string, and skin. Courtesy of the Royal British Columbia Museum, Victoria, British Columbia, Canada. #10665.*

### ABOUT THE MEDIA

The Haida use red cedar to make their masks. The pink wood is easy to split and carve. At times, they also use yellow cedar and white alder wood for masks. Some masks are trimmed with feathers, shells, or copper.

### ABOUT THE TECHNIQUE

Most Haida craftsmen create their own tools. Some carving tools have stone blades, while others have blades of shell or steel. Besides chisels, carvers use simple drills that they rotate between their palms. They give their work a smooth finish by rubbing it with fine sandstone or sharkskin.

# Votive Horse

## About the Artist

The identity of the Indian artist who created *Votive Horse* is unknown. India, a huge nation in South Asia, has been isolated from the rest of the Asian continent by the Himalayas. This geographic separation has limited the influence of China and the Middle East on the arts of India. Nearly 70 percent of India's population still lives in rural villages, where traditional art flourishes.

### ABOUT ART HISTORY

Today, as well as in the past, Indian villagers pay potters to make clay horses and elephants for them. Often the figures are part of festivals. Villagers place the statues on the many outdoor shrines throughout India. A shrine might be near a sacred pond or under a tree. These statues are offerings to the gods, thanking them for their blessings or asking them for favors. The statues are called "votive" because they are being offered to a religious figure. The votive horse often symbolizes a spirit that has been freed from its human body and is becoming nearer to perfection. As soon as the statue is offered, it has served its purpose. No one tries to preserve it. Soon the clay offerings disintegrate in the sun and rain, and the villagers replace them.

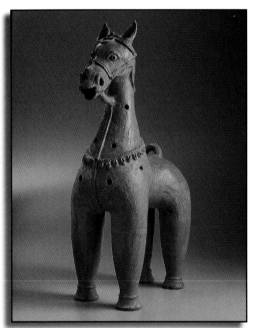

*Artist Unknown. (India).* Votive Horse. *Clay. From the Girard Foundation Collection, in the Museum of International Folk Art, a unit of the Museum of New Mexico, Santa Fe, New Mexico. Photographer: Michel Monteaux.*

### ABOUT THE ARTWORK

The terra cotta horses produced for shrines are often more than a yard tall. Smaller ones are often made as toys. Huge terra cotta horses, more than 16 feet tall, guard some villages. The horses are decorated according to the traditions of that village or region. Some of today's potters adapt their designs to please customers.

### ABOUT THE MEDIA

Terra cotta is a raw clay that has been fired without being glazed. Clay is one of the main building materials in India. The walls and roofs of many village homes, along with cooking pots and plates, are made of clay.

### ABOUT THE TECHNIQUE

Terra cotta horses are made by joining the head, neck, body, and legs, which are created separately.

# Delaware Shoulder Bag

## About the Artist

The Indian Removal Act of 1830 forced many Native American groups to leave their homelands. The Delaware nation was pushed from homes in the Delaware and Ohio River valleys to land west of the Mississippi. Formerly, farmers, hunters, and fishers living in wooded areas and lush river valleys had to find ways to live on prairie land in Nebraska, Kansas, and Oklahoma. As in most Native American societies, the Delaware women were responsible for caring for the children, cooking, housekeeping, gardening, and creating their families' pots, baskets, and clothing.

### ABOUT ART HISTORY

After the Delaware's relocation to the prairie, the women combined the traditional square shape of their shoulder bags with bead embroidery. They also widened the shoulder strap. The Delaware women helped develop the "prairie style" of beadwork. This was a combination of designs from several Native American cultures. For the prairie style, they filled in open areas between the designs with vibrant, contrasting colors. They often created a "negative" design on the bags.

*Artist unknown. Delaware Tribe (United States).* Delaware Shoulder Bag. *c. 1860. Wool and cotton fabric. 21.9 × 19.7 cm. Detroit Institute of Arts, Detroit, Michigan. Photograph © 1996 Detroit Institute of Arts, Founders Society Purchase.*

### ABOUT THE ARTWORK

Shoulder bags were worn by men at ceremonial events, to show off the skills of the Delaware craftswomen.

### ABOUT THE MEDIA

The shoulder bags were made from wool and cotton fabric, silk ribbon, and glass beads.

### ABOUT THE TECHNIQUE

The Delaware women used bold designs in their beadwork, placed the designs close together, and outlined them in white. The designs were abstract and symmetrical, with each side a mirror image of the other.

# Gui Ritual Food Container

## About the Artist

The ancient Chinese used bronze containers during their religious ceremonies or rituals. The containers were also symbols of political power. The craftsmen who made them were well-respected. Some of the containers were buried with the dead, while others were buried as offerings to the natural spirits of the rivers and mountains. Still other containers were carefully hidden. When they were dug up or found, sometimes generations later, they were treasured as links to the past. These containers now serve as a record of ancient Chinese culture and proof of the skill of its artists.

### ABOUT ART HISTORY

The "bronze age" in China lasted nearly 1,000 years. Each period of the bronze age produced a variety of styles of containers. Each style has a different name, different characteristics, and a different purpose. There are more than 100 types and names of containers from the bronze age. The first ancient ritual food container was offered for sale in the early twentieth century and was probably produced during the eleventh century B.C.

*Artist unknown. (China).* Gui Ritual Food Container (Zhou Dynasty). *Eleventh century B.C. Bronze. Courtesy of the Arthur M. Sackler Gallery, Smithsonian Institution, Washington, DC.*

containers produced during the Western Zhou period, 1050–771 B.C. were decorated with long-tailed birds that looked like peacocks. Later, these birds were stylized and became bands of patterns that circled the container. Long inscriptions on some of the containers recorded important historical information.

### ABOUT THE MEDIA

All ritual food containers were made of bronze.

### ABOUT THE ARTWORK

Ancient bronze containers were shaped according to their uses. Besides the round, wide-mouthed ritual food containers, there were narrow-necked wine containers and shallow water basins. The designs on the containers were symbolic, but their meanings are often unclear to us. Many of the bronze

### ABOUT THE TECHNIQUE

By the time of the Western Zhou dynasty, craftsmen no longer created containers by beating cold bronze into shape. Instead, they made a mold from clay and carved the design they wanted into it. Then, they poured melted bronze into the mold. When it cooled, the container needed only polishing.

# Egyptian Mummy Case

## About the Artist

Ancient Egyptians believed that each person had a soul and an invisible twin. Both would live in a tomb after their death. People would be able to live forever if their soul and their invisible twin could recognize their body after it was dead. That is why bodies had to be preserved, or mummified. If their bodies were destroyed, the people would not have eternal life. At first, the Egyptians simply buried their dead, and the hot, dry climate preserved the bodies. In time, they learned to embalm, or mummify, the bodies before burial. The mummies of powerful people, such as pharaohs or kings, were placed in mummy cases. The cases were painted with images of gods and goddesses that would protect the dead person in his or her next life. Many mummy cases included an inner coffin in the shape of the mummy and an outer coffin. This combination was then placed inside a stone container called a sarcophagus. If the dead person had been powerful or wealthy, each container would be decorated. The sarcophagus of a king was then buried in a tomb, and a pyramid was built over it as a monument to his power.

## ABOUT ART HISTORY

Art styles did not change much over the centuries in ancient Egypt. Figures and symbols were placed in a line, with little attempt at showing depth. All figures were rigid, shown from the front or side, with little variation. Some critics think this lack of change reflects the Egyptian belief that life does not change, even after death.

## ABOUT THE ARTWORK

The inside of the mummy case was painted with images of gods and goddesses of the underworld. The outside was often covered by hieroglyphs, ancient picture-letters

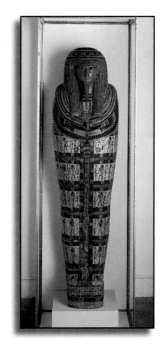

*Artist unknown. (Egypt).* Egyptian Mummy Case. *Wood. The Brooklyn Museum, New York, New York. The Charles Edwin Wilbour Fund (#35.1265)*

that recorded spells to help the dead person in his or her next life. The head of the mummy case was formed into a sculpture of the dead person, emphasizing his or her strength or beauty. Other images on the outside of the case indicated the person's status in society.

## ABOUT THE MEDIA

Inner coffins were made from wood or plaster; the outer sarcophagus was made from stone. The inner coffin of a king might be decorated with gold, enamel, and semiprecious stones, such as turquoise and lapis lazuli.

# Sash

## About the Artist

The Osage are Native Americans who once hunted buffalo and gathered food on the prairie. They lived on the land that is now called Arkansas, Kansas, Missouri, and Oklahoma. After government treaties took most of their land, the Osage moved to a reservation in Oklahoma and became farmers. In the late 1800s, oil was discovered on their reservation, bringing great wealth to the Osage community. Some Osage craftswomen continue to weave and create traditional clothing. On ceremonial occasions, the Osage still wear traditional garments. Some of the garments the women have created now hang in museums and in private art collections.

## ABOUT ART HISTORY

One popular image of Native Americans in terms of clothing is that of the Plains Indian dressed in buffalo hide or buckskin decorated with beadwork, a war bonnet, and war paint. This style of dress, though, is only one of many. Other popular clothing materials were furs and cotton and other plant materials. Contact with non-Native American cultures also brought new materials and clothing designs to the Plains.

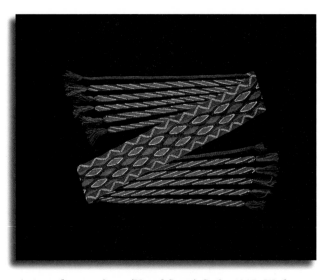

*Artist unknown.* Osage (United States). Sash. 1885. Wool yarn and glass beads. 213.7 cm. Detroit Institute of Arts, Detroit, Michigan. Photograph ©1996 Detroit Institute of Arts, Founders Society Purchase.

## ABOUT THE ARTWORK

Osage sashes can be worn around the head, neck, or waist. They are woven in a range of patterns, such as double arrow, lightning and arrow, and chevron. A sash might end in short clusters of fringe or in fringe that hangs as long as 25 inches and is braided with beads. The artists continue Osage traditions by using strong color contrasts.

## ABOUT THE MEDIA

Early Osage sashes were made by twisting together strands of plant material, buffalo hair, and coyote and rabbit fur. In time, craftswomen began using materials, such as wool yarn and glass beads.

## ABOUT THE TECHNIQUE

The Osage artists weave sashes with their fingers, just as they always have. Long ago, when the Osage began trading with the Europeans, the Osage women traded for tools to make sashes and other traditional garments. These tools included steel scissors and needles, thread, and sewing machines.

## About the Artist

The Chinese artist of *Sakyamuni Buddha* and the Gandharan artist of *Seated Buddha* are unknown. Buddha was a religious teacher whose image has been the subject of much artwork in Asia. At first, followers of Buddha were forbidden from portraying him in a physical form. Instead, they had to represent him with footprints or with symbols of life, such as the lotus blossom. The Buddha image now represents peace and harmony, with Buddhist art reflecting the cultures of its followers.

### ABOUT ART HISTORY

Buddhism began in India about 600–500 B.C. Its founder, Siddhartha Gautama, was known as Buddha, or "Awakened One." Buddhism spread to Gandhara, now western Pakistan, during the third century B.C. Gandhara was also occupied by Greek armies for a short time during this period. The Gandharan *Seated Buddha* has characteristics of Roman sculpture. For example, his face resembles Apollo, and he is dressed like Roman statues. The Chinese *Sakyamuni Buddha* was based on a Gandharan Buddha.

*Artist unknown.* (Gandhara, Pakistan). Seated Buddha. *Schist. $12\frac{3}{4} \times 8\frac{7}{8}$ inches. Asian Art Museum of San Francisco/The Avery Brundage Collection.*

thinner and lighter, showing the shapes of the bodies underneath. The folds in the robes of *Sakyamuni Buddha* form a balanced, symmetrical pattern.

### ABOUT THE MEDIA

Early Gandharan Buddhas were carved from wood. Later ones were made from stone, and stucco was often used after A.D. 300. Early Chinese Buddhas were shaped from clay and mud. Later ones were carved from stone or cast in bronze. Still later, Chinese Buddhas were made from ceramics.

### ABOUT THE ARTWORK

The Buddha sculptures vary slightly. For example, the robe of the *Seated Buddha* falls unevenly over his shoulders in heavy folds. Chinese Buddhas wore robes that were

### ABOUT THE TECHNIQUE

Techniques for creating Buddhas ranged from shaping stone with chisels and mallets to casting bronze in molds. Many statues were painted, gilded, or glazed.